bed

a play with music by Sheila Callaghan

ABOUT THE AUTHOR

Sheila Callaghan's plays have been produced and developed with Soho Rep, Playwright's Horizons, Yale Rep, South Coast Repertory, Clubbed Thumb, The LARK, Actor's Theatre of Louisville, New Georges, The Flea, Woolly Mammoth, Boston Court, and Rattlestick Playwright's Theatre, among others. Sheila is the recipient of the Princess Grace Award for emerging artists, a Jerome Fellowship from the Playwright's Center in Minneapolis, a MacDowell Residency, a Cherry Lane Mentorship Fellowship, the Susan Smith Blackburn Award, and the prestigious Whiting Award. Her plays have been produced internationally in New Zealand, Australia, Norway, Germany, Portugal, and the Czech Republic. These include SCAB, CRAWL FADE TO WHITE, CRUMBLE (Lay Me Down, Justin Timberlake), WE ARE NOT THESE HANDS, DEAD CITY, LASCIVIOUS SOMETHING, KATE CRACKERNUTS, THAT PRETTY PRETTY; OR, THE RAPE PLAY, FEVER/DREAM, EVERYTHING YOU TOUCH, ROADKILL CONFIDENTIAL, ELEVADA, BED, and WOMEN LAUGHING ALONE WITH SALAD. She is published with Playscripts.com and Samuel French, and several of her collected works are published with Counterpoint Press. She has taught playwriting at Columbia University, The University of Rochester, The College of New Jersey, Florida State University, and Spalding University. Sheila is an affiliated artist with Clubbed Thumb and a member of the Obie winning playwright's organization 13P. Sheila is also an alumni of New Dramatists.

In 2010, Callaghan was profiled by Marie Claire as one of "18 Successful Women Who Are Changing the World." She was also named one of Variety magazine's "10 Screenwriters to Watch" of 2010. Sheila was a longtime writer/producer on the hit Showtime comedy *Shameless* and a founder of the feminist activist group The Kilroys. She was nominated for a 2016 Golden Globe for her work on the Hulu comedy series *Casual* and a 2017 WGA Award for her Shameless episode "I Am A Storm."

Please visit her at **www.sheilacallaghan.com**. She's waiting for you.

Copyright © 2019 by Sheila Callaghan
All Rights Reserved

BED is fully protected under the copyright laws of the United States of America, the British Commonwealth, including Canada, and all other countries of the Copyright Union. All rights, including professional and amateur stage productions, recitation, lecturing, public reading, motion picture, radio broadcasting, television and the rights of translation into foreign languages are strictly reserved.

For all <u>production inquiries</u>,
please contact Ally Schuster at
Creative Artists Agency
405 Lexington Avenue, 19th Floor
New York, NY 10010
ph: 212.277.9000

Print edition
ISBN: 978-1-7341402-0-0

tripwireharlot.com
savagecandy.com

CAUTION: Professional and amateur producers are hereby warned that *BED* is subject to a licensing fee. Publication of this play(s) does not imply availability for performance. Both amateurs and professionals considering a production are strongly advised to contact Tripwire Harlot Press before starting rehearsals, advertising, or booking a theatre. A licensing fee must be paid whether the title(s) is presented for charity or gain and whether or not admission is charged. Professional/ Stock licensing fees are quoted upon application.

No one shall make any changes in this title(s) for the purpose of production. No part of this book may be reproduced, stored in a retrieval system, or transmitted in any form, by any means, now known or yet to be invented, including mechanical, electronic, photocopying, recording, videotaping, or otherwise, without the prior written permission of the publisher. No one shall upload this title(s), or part of this title(s), to any social media websites.

For all inquiries regarding motion picture, television, and other media rights, please contact Tripwire Harlot Press: info@tripwireharlot.com.

BED was first presented at the Echo Theater Company in Los Angeles on February 6, 2016. The performance was directed by Jennifer Chambers, with sets by Se Oh, costumes by Michael Mullen, lights by Sean Mallory, and sound by Jeff Gardner. Original compositions and songs were written by Sophocles Papavasilopouolos and Maxwell Gualtieri. The Production Stage Manager was Samantha McCann. The cast was as follows:

HOLLY . . . . Kate Morgan Chadwick
CLIFF . . . . TW Leshner
JC . . . . Johnathan McClain

KATE MORGAN CHADWICK AND TW LESHNER IN A SCENE FROM *BED*. PHOTO CREDIT: DARRETT SANDERS

CHARACTERS
HOLLY
CLIFF
JC

TIME
now-ish

SETTING(S)
New York City, Minneapolis, Berlin, Los Angeles, Paris.

AUTHOR'S NOTE
The play takes pace over 10 years and should run less than 90 minutes.

In the center of the stage: a bed. It glows eerily. Sound hums, throbs. Bed seems to float ominously.

A WOMAN age 30-35, dressed only in a slip, crawls towards the bed from very far away, perhaps from the street, from outside the theatre. Crawls on her forearms and elbows and belly and knees, slowly like a lizard. A blind animal. She knows the way by scent. Or habit. Or ritual. Maybe her knees are dirty, her elbows, her chin.

She crawls towards the bed. The light on the bed intensifies. As does the sound around it. Grows to a deafening roar. She crawls in the center of the bed. Slowly rises onto her knees. Pulls at her slip. Exposes her neck. Bares her claws, her fangs.

Suddenly, the lights snap to a soft evening ambience. The woman (HOLLY) giggles and throws the covers over her head.

   CLIFF., also 30-35, enters. Sees her lump beneath the bed. Smiles. Waits a moment. Looks around the room. She giggles again. He still waits.

HOLLY.
What are you waiting for

CLIFF.
These paintings are great
you do all of ' em?

HOLLY.
Yes!
Get over here!

                He comes closer.

HOLLY.
Stop!

                He stops. She peeks out from
                beneath the covers.

HOLLY.
I'm kinda drunk
I might have whiskey dick

CLIFF.
Girls get...?

HOLLY.
It just might take me longer to come
I'm usually pretty quick

CLIFF.
Ok
I don't really drink

HOLLY.
I had three wines at the party then a vodka soda at the bar then two shots at the second bar

CLIFF.
Impressive--

HOLLY.
PANTS!

> Cliff undoes his belt. Folds it carefully, lays it to the side.

HOLLY.
Do people call you Cliffy?

CLIFF.
Just Cliff.
Like falling off a.

HOLLY.
Like the friendly dog
Like the big red dog.

CLIFF.
Sure

> Cliff slides off his pants. Beneath are tighty whities.

CLIFF.
I have better underpants at home
They go lower on the thigh
I didn't expect this or I woulda

HOLLY.
You have ostrich legs

CLIFF.
My brother used to say that!
He totally used to / say that

HOLLY.
SHIRT!

> He slides off his shirt.

HOLLY.
God you're skinny
You look like Jesus

CLIFF.
Uh

HOLLY.
It's cool
I wanted to fuck Jesus when I was sixteen
Underpants
Please

                          Beat. Cliff slides off his underpants.

CLIFF.
Holly
I don't usually

HOLLY.
Should we not?

CLIFF.
No I want to
I just, this isn't

HOLLY.
I get it
We can go slower
We can snuggle
We can talk

CLIFF.
No it's ok

HOLLY.
Let's talk a little
sooooo

HOLLY. (cont)
How many languages do you speak

CLIFF.
Four

HOLLY.
Four?
Fuck you

CLIFF.
I'm only really fluent in French and English
I have some Latin and some German

HOLLY.
Why?
Why do you have all those?

CLIFF.
My mother is French so.
My brother moved there
Um German I learned because of my undergrad degree

HOLLY.
In what?

CLIFF.
German.
And fiction.
wanted to write novels like the Germanic modernists
Like, you know.

HOLLY.
Uh-huh

CLIFF.
melancholy, apocalyptic, symbolist / whatever

HOLLY.
Sure

> Holly begins jerking him off beneath the covers.

HOLLY.
Say some German stuff
Some bad evil shit
Some Nazi shit

CLIFF.
Um
Ok um
"Juden sind eine Geißel! Wir müssen sie zu beseitigen!"

HOLLY.
that was terrifying
What was it

CLIFF.
Um
"Jews are a scourge, we must eliminate them!"

> Stops jerking.

HOLLY.
You're a fucking Anti-semite?

CLIFF.
What? No! You asked me to—

HOLLY.
I'm kidding!

> Continues jerking.

CLIFF.
Oh

CLIFF. (cont)
Ok
Oohh
man

HOLLY.
Yeah?

CLIIFF
God you're
Good at that
What about you
languages

HOLLY.
Only one unfortch

CLIFF.
Tell me other stuff
About you

HOLLY.
Nah

CLIFF.
Simple stuff
Your parents

HOLLY.
My father is a cork board
My mother is a lawnmower

CLIFF.
Real stuff

HOLLY.
I own a Bill Clinton ceramic ashtray
I love popping zits on people's backs
I'm a shitty driver

HOLLY. (cont)
I laugh when I get emotional
My father jerked off on me when I was fifteen

CLIFF.
Whoa—

HOLLY.
I hate pizza and people who dress their cats for Halloween
NOW WOULD YOU PLEASE FUCK ME.

CLIFF.
Can I go down on you first?

HOLLY.
I'm expecting my period

CLIFF.
I don't care

HOLLY.
I'm not sure how clean I am

CLIFF.
I don't / care

>He puts his head beneath the sheets. She yanks him back up, flips him onto his back, straddles him, and rides him hard.

CLIFF.
Whoa
Easy

HOLLY.
I
Said
No

HOLLY. (cont)
Fucker

> She rides him until he climaxes, which is rather quickly. Then she flips over, grabs a tissue, and wipes herself beneath the sheets.

CLIFF.
I'm sorry—

HOLLY.
Ride-or-die baby
I'll whack off in the morning

CLIFF.
Okay

HOLLY.
You can crash here if you need to
My roommate doesn't give a shit
She always has naked dudes walking in and out of the living room

CLIFF.
Ok

> Holly grabs her guitar.

HOLLY.
You're all right, Cliffy
I don't care what they say about ya

> Holly plays a fierce lick.

CLIFF.
What who says

HOLLY.
No one
It's just something I say

CLIFF.
wanna know what they say about you?

HOLLY.
Who?

CLIFF.
Julie
She said you were a little crazy
And a genius

HOLLY.
That's so condescending
Everyone is a genius
Dogs are geniuses
Tables are geniuses

CLIFF.
You get called that a lot?

HOLLY.
Who doesn't

CLIFF.
Me, for one
Maybe when I was a kid

HOLLY.
What else did she say

CLIFF.
That I was gonna fall in love with you

HOLLY.
What an idiot

CLIFF.
And that you're unhappy

HOLLY.
I have Chronic Loneliness
It's a Very Serious Condition
I could die from it

CLIFF.
Could you wait til I leave first?

HOLLY.
What if you never leave

CLIFF.
Then I guess you'll have to stay alive

>   Cliff begins to get her off with his hand beneath the sheets.

HOLLY.
Oh
Jesus

CLIFF.
Yeah?

HOLLY.
You
Mother
Fucking

CLIFF.
You're
So
beautiful

>   He puts his head beneath the sheets

>and goes down on her. She ramps up quickly.

HOLLY.
YOU
FUCKING
ASSHOLE
JESUS
FUUUCK
GOD
FUCK
YOOOOOUUUUAAAHHH

>She climaxes hard and immediately bursts into tears. Cliff comes up for air, terrified.

CLIFF.
Jesus
What'd I do?

HOLLY.
Nothing
You're great

CLIFF.
Are you okay?

HOLLY.
This happens sometimes
With new people
It's ok

>She blows her nose.

CLIFF.
Are you sure?

HOLLY.
Yeah
It's like
I dunno vulnerability or something
Sorry

CLIFF.
It's okay

> She hands him a tissue. He wipes his mouth.

HOLLY.
Anyway I'm usually faster

CLIFF.
That was

HOLLY.
Hair trigger
Tripwire harlot

CLIFF.
Hot

HOLLY.
There's a candy cane stuck to my ass

CLIFF.
What

HOLLY.
I'm always finding shit in this bed

CLIFF.
It's summer

HOLLY.
I never wash my sheets

                Small beat.

CLIFF.
How many dudes have been here since the last time you washed

HOLLY.
None of your fucking business

                She unwraps the candy cane and sucks on it.

HOLLY. (cont)
I'm still drunk

CLIFF.
I like you

                Holly passes out with the candy cane in her mouth.

                She scratches herself with her hand. Scratches her body like a dog with fleas. He watches her.

                Lights snap, or stutter, or blink, or something. He pushes on her. Hands her a Styrofoam container of noodles. She eats.

HOLLY.
Shut up
You've only had three girlfriends?

CLIFF.
And one horrendous one night stand

HOLLY.
Why horrendous

CLIFF.
It was an internet hookup
We negotiated sex before we met

HOLLY.
What about the others

CLIFF.
College girlfriend
Then Renee the Ann Arbor grad student
And then this social worker who had a bizarre obsession with baby camels

HOLLY.
If you've only nailed four chicks
how come you're so good at fucking?

CLIFF.
I'm not
I'm just good at fucking you.

HOLLY.
What else are you good at?

CLIFF.
Cooking.

HOLLY.
What!
You cook and you're making us eat this shit?

CLIFF.
I have some dishes.
Fish, stews
I have a nice collection of Le Creuset

HOLLY.
Why don't I know this?

CLIFF.
I'm rationing my virtues

HOLLY.
I LOVE BEING FED
Feed me!
Tonight!

CLIFF.
Ah
My brother is still at my place, so
He's in town from Paris

HOLLY.
Oh cool
I'd love to meet him.

>   Small beat.

CLIFF.
Um sure.

HOLLY.
What

CLIFF.
No I said sure

HOLLY.
Is there something wrong with him?
Is he like

CLIFF.
No

HOLLY.
Aspergersey, or

CLIFF.
No no no
I don't
I don't
bring people around very often

HOLLY.
So?
I'm mostly harmless

CLIFF.
Well that's debatable
I feel harmed by you, a little
In a good way
But.
Um

> Small beat.

CLIFF.
You know actually it's totally fine

HOLLY.
Forget it

CLIFF.
No I want to
It'll be good for me

HOLLY.
"Good for you?" Okay.

CLIFF.
No, that's not what I / meant

HOLLY.
You're embarrassed of me--

CLIFF.
No!
It's just

HOLLY.
Stop talking

CLIFF.
Why? It's fine!
I'll text him now--

HOLLY.
Seriously
Could you just
maybe
Go?

CLIFF.
Why?

HOLLY.
And take this shit with you

CLIFF.
Holly

HOLLY.
Go, Cliff
Go
Leave
Not joking

CLIFF.
What is this

She grabs her headphones. Begins

> singing to herself as Cliff dresses himself.

CLIFF. (cont.)
Will I call you?

> Holly flips him off and sings louder. He exits. She gets through as much of the song as possible in a very entertaining way. Then. Lights snap, or stutter, or blink. Cliff returns and climbs on top of Holly, fucking her vigorously. They climax hard, at the same time.

HOLLY.
Simultaneous, bitches!!

CLIFF.
Had to conjure my old ethics professor in a sports bra for that one

> They snuggle. He smells her hair.

CLIFF.
Yuck. Cigarettes

HOLLY.
Go suck multiple dicks

CLIFF.
I missed you
I've been stalking your Myspace page
You bought a new backpack

HOLLY.
Target

CLIFF.
You've been drunk a lot

HOLLY.
I've been coping

CLIFF.
Who's the tall dude with the old-timey spectacles
The one with all the tattoos

HOLLY.
Um

CLIFF.
I don't want to know.
I don't, right?

HOLLY.
No

CLIFF.
Ok
What else did I miss

HOLLY.
I got a job offer.
My old housemate is touring Japan with her metal band
She needs me to cover her for a year

CLIFF.
Doing what

HOLLY.
Teaching music at a school for gifted kids

CLIFF.
That's terrific
Where

HOLLY.
Minneapolis

CLIFF.
As in
The city?

HOLLY.
Yeah

CLIFF.
Are you gonna do it

HOLLY.
Yeah
Apartments are like, a third of the price
And they have a rad music scene
And it pays well

CLIFF.
Sounds great

HOLLY.
Yeah

CLIFF.
Why am I here.

HOLLY.
Because I called you

CLIFF.
Why did you call me

>Holly reaches inside the bed. Pulls out a small canvas. Cliff examines it.

HOLLY.
It's new.

CLIFF.
Is that a—

HOLLY.
Nutsack.
Yeah.

CLIFF.
And this?

HOLLY.
A tongue.
With miniature tongues growing out of it.

CLIFF.
Is this an ostrich

HOLLY.
It is

CLIFF.
(moved)
You rendered me.

HOLLY.
I'm in there too
You can't tell
It's this thing
This shitty little dot

CLIFF.
Holly

HOLLY.
What?
Uh oh

CLIFF.
I love you.

HOLLY.
Oh.
Rad.

                Lights change.

                HOLLY. breathes out. A giant cloud of breath fills the room, the stage, the theatre.

HOLLY.
JESUS FUCKING CHRIST did you see that?
My breath.
Indoors.

CLIFF.
When are they fixing the thing again?

HOLLY.
They said noon
Mother fuck.
I'm wearing every single sock I own

CLIFF.
we're forced to use body heat
like eskimos

HOLLY.
We can't ever leave the bed
We'll get frostbite and die

CLIFF.
Ok but my flight leaves on Sunday

HOLLY.
Fuck your flight

CLIFF.
I gotta work the next day

HOLLY.
Fuck your job
My boss owns this douchey club in the North Loop
He'll set you up with a bartending gig

CLIFF.
I hate bars

HOLLY.
Do it for the material
drunk idiots bloviating about tax reform and national security?
It writes itself
OH MY GOD
We have to go to the Mall of America before you leave
Did you know they have a bar that serves discontinued breakfast cereals?
You can get a whole bowl of marbits

CLIFF.
Of what?

HOLLY.
marshmellow bits
like the lucky charms
They have a movie theatre too
And old school video games
And a bar
We could do Jäger bombs and play Qbert--

CLIFF.
Why don't you ever talk to your family

HOLLY.
…

CLIFF.
Or even about them

HOLLY.
Um. Daddy issues?

CLIFF.
Yeah but. Not even extended family

HOLLY.
Dunno.

CLIFF.
You're untethered

HOLLY.
sure

CLIFF.
You don't see how scary that is?

HOLLY.
For who?

CLIFF.
both of us

HOLLY.
Dude
We have three more days together
Could you just like
Pause the tragedy til you leave?

CLIFF.
I mean fundamentally, we're like
I'll always be floating on this like

CLIFF. (cont)
Raft of trepidation
And you'll always be tugging it

HOLLY.
So?

CLIFF.
Why doesn't that bother you?

HOLLY.
Because I dig you fool

CLIFF.
But do you need me?

HOLLY.
Why do I need to need you?

CLIFF.
Because
Oh lord
This is
hard

HOLLY.
Are you
god
are you breaking up with me?

CLIFF.
No I'm
I think I'm doing the opposite
Goddamn it

HOLLY.
Oh

CLIFF.
I wanted there to be like
I dunno

HOLLY.
Fuck, man

CLIFF.
Mariachis

HOLLY.
Shut the fuck up

CLIFF.
Ok.
I take it back

HOLLY.
You can't take it back
Words don't work that way

CLIFF.
I didn't use words
I *implied.*

HOLLY.
You can't take an *implication* back

> Holly pulls out a flask from the bed and takes a belt.

CLIFF.
not even noon

HOLLY.
It's a fucking blowtorch

CLIFF.
What

HOLLY.
Marriage, asshole
it melts you down into a puddle

CLIFF.
Blowtorch

HOLLY.
No edges!
no definition!

CLIFF.
You make your own definition—

HOLLY.
All the shit that's supposed to hold you up--

CLIFF.
I mean
ideally
You hold each other up

HOLLY.
That does not happen
Not in real life

CLIFF.
It does though

HOLLY.
NO IT DOESN'T
HUMANS ARE DESIGNED TO BE ALONE
WHO THE FUCK ARE WE TO DEFY THE NATURAL ORDER

CLIFF.
Holly

HOLLY.
I'm gonna start laughing now
I can feel it coming
It's gonna be scary

CLIFF.
Ok

> Holly begins laughing uncontrollably. It's scary. It goes on and on and on. It ebs and flows. Once it seems like it's ending, it starts again. That happens a few times. Add some howling and some snarling. Cliff watches, scared at first, then curious. When it finally ends, Holly takes a deep breath, then takes a belt of her flask. She's calm now, like nothing ever happened.

HOLLY.
I am
A
Really
Bad
Person
And at some point
I'm gonna need you to punish me for it
So.
As long as we're clear.

CLIFF.
We're clear

HOLLY.
Fine.

> Holly stands on the bed. During the following, she wraps herself in the

> sheet. She assembles a bouquet made of garbage: candy wrappers, used coffee filters, yogurt containers, a beer bottle, cigarette butts, takeout containers, plastic utensils, prescription bottles, etc. Finally, she uses the pillowcase for a veil.
>
> A voice is heard, a priest's voice, on mike.

VOICE
Tu aimeras cet homme pour toujours.
Il te décevra.
Mais tu lui pardonneras.
Il te décevra de nouveau.
Tu te demanderas alors si cela se répétera ainsi sans fin.
Il ne t'aimera qu'avec les parties de lui-même qu'il croit disponibles à l'amour.
Tu l'aimeras avec les parties de toi que tu ne possèdes même pas.
Vous connaîtrez tour-à-tour un bonnheur délirant et un gouffre de désespoir.
Vous partagerez ensemble plus que ce que vous n'aviez cru possible.
Mais vous demeurez quand même des étrangers l'un pour l'autre.
Voilà le chemin qui s'ouvre devant vous à partir de ce jour.

> Holly eats the whole mess. Cliff watches. Beat. Lights change.

CLIFF.
Did you see how wasted my brother got?

HOLLY.
He kept looking at me with this *face*
Like he was dissecting a fetal pig

CLIFF.
That's just his face

HOLLY.
But now we're BFF's
the Jäger bombs probably helped
what were you and your dad talking about?

CLIFF.
He's worried I'm putting my Ivy League Education to waste

HOLLY.
Does he know about your novel?
Does he know about the writer's colony?

CLIFF.
I'll tell him when I'm holding the galleys in my fat little fingers

                        She crawls on top of him.

HOLLY.
Hey
You *own* me now

CLIFF.
Such a feminist

HOLLY.
I can't wait to go to restaurants
 "My *spouse* will have the shrimp"

CLIFF.
No one says that

HOLLY.
And she'll be all,
Damn.
Guess that chick's off the market

CLIFF.
Our waitress is a lesbian

HOLLY.
And she'll slip you her number
And say
Call me anyway
And she'll come to our pad in a big dumb sweatshirt and fluorescent leggings
And we'll open a bottle of wine
And finish it too quick
she'll start to take off her clothes
I'll go, wait.
Let him do it.
And you peel off her leggings very slowly
And beneath, she has on these like
Bondage panties
Like black with leather straps and a pussy harness
And you slip your fingers inside her
And she's so fucking wet
And you go down on her for like an hour
And she comes eighty times
And I just.
Watch.

CLIFF.
You don't wanna join in

HOLLY.
And eventually
You send her packing
And the second she leaves
I fuck you stupid

CLIFF.
Best marriage ever

> They begin making love. He stops

>   abruptly.

CLIFF. (cont)
What if the only reason we did this
is 'cause we like having sex with each other

HOLLY.
I don't see a problem with that

CLIFF.
But what happens when stuff goes wrong?

HOLLY.
We bang it out

CLIFF.
Good plan

>   He grabs his phone and types.

HOLLY.
What are you doing?

CLIFF.
Setting my alarm

HOLLY.
Don't bother
my anxiety will throttle us awake

CLIFF.
It's not a reliable system

HOLLY.
How often do I sleep past six-thirty

CLIFF.
I don't wanna miss our flight

HOLLY.
We'll catch another
Kawaii isn't going anywhere
Neither is the airport
Neither is consumer travel
We have the rest of our lives to worry about that shit

CLIFF.
What should we worry about now?

HOLLY.
Nothing
Not sunburns
Not flipflops
Not crappy surfer motels
We're inside a soap bubble
floating

> They're both getting drowsy.

CLIFF.
Yeah

HOLLY.
We're made of breath
A child's breath

CLIFF.
Yeah

HOLLY.
Sugar sours
Chocolate milk

CLIFF.
Yeah

> Beat. Drowsier.

HOLLY.
Cough syrup
rain

> Long beat.

....summer

> They are asleep. Then. She springs
> up. Prowls around him. Pauses at the
> edge of the bed. Stares at him. And
> stares. And stares. Time passes, she's
> still staring.
>
> Then removes large headphones
> from the bed and a guitar. Cliff rises,
> begins typing furiously on a laptop.
> They both work it out for a bit.
>
> Cliff reads aloud to himself.

CLIFF.
"He pours endless rivers of booze
Into the mouths of those who seem to know no end to the revelry
A perpetual-motion machine of vibrating humans
Blinding each other with the glints of their sequins

> He stops abruptly. Notices Holly
> chewing on the cord of her
> headphones. Beat. Continues
> typing.

CLIFF. (cont)
He thinks of April in their bed
beat up Les Paul on her lap
Chewing on the cord of her headphones"

> Beat. He pokes her. She whips off her

headphones.

HOLLY.
Productivity motherfuckers
Where you at

CLIFF.
Felix's first night bartending
It's still too labored
I want it to have like *gravitas*
Like the german expressionists
Whatever
How's yours going

HOLLY.
I think I found it

CLIFF.
Play it

> She plays a phrase for 2-4 measures.

HOLLY.
…and then this fuzz bass comes in, like this…

> She plays the same guitar line and sings over it.

HOLLY. (cont)
…and then - this is the one - we bring in a ring-modulated Rhodes doubling a distorted B3 and it all breaks loose…

> She sings the Rhodes/B3 layer over the guitar - maybe switching to sing the fuzz bass to emphasize that they're all playing at the same time. Sings it out. It's gorgeous. Beat. She looks at Cliff expectantly.

HOLLY. (cont)
Yeah?

CLIFF.
You're a genius

HOLLY.
I am!

CLIFF.
I married a genius

HOLLY.
You did!

CLIFF.
Life is good!

HOLLY.
It is!
Last night I dreamed I gave birth to a Shetland pony
I kept him on the roof of your Brooklyn apartment
and fed him dead bees
And when I woke up this morning?
This odd phrase was lodged in my head
"her daughter's school board is up to no good"
that's what this song is about

CLIFF.
bees or school boards?

HOLLY.
Motherhood, dummy

CLIFF.
Really?

HOLLY.
don't get a dad boner
I still hate babies

CLIFF.
Even though you talk about them constantly

HOLLY.
No I talk about motherhood
Babies are awful.
drunk little hairless possums

CLIFF.
Well I'm ready

HOLLY.
you wanna be elbow deep in someone else's shit?
go work in a nursing home

CLIFF.
When we got home from the bar the other night?
And you were reeeaaaallly drunk?
You told me you wanted a little girl

HOLLY.
No I didn't

CLIFF.
You absolutely did
You said you wanted to name her Jackalope

HOLLY.
you have no proof
but that's a fucking great name

CLIFF.
You don't think you deserve it
it's something other people get to have
People who've been taught how to love properly

>   Holly grabs her guitar.

HOLLY.
Stop sussing me, bro

CLIFF.
You're just pissed I know you better than *you* do --

HOLLY.
Fuck babies.
Fuck them in their stupid fucking faces.

>   Holly shreds for a bit. Lights snap, or
>   stutter, or blink, or something. Holly
>   trades the guitar for a newborn. She
>   addresses it.

HOLLY.
my teacup
my shucked oyster
my carbomb

your mouse-cries sift over me like dry rice
you have two souls
one is mild and fine-spun
the other arrogant and histrionic
I can't tell which is closer to the truth
But I suppose that's not for me to judge

I have two things to tell you
One is a secret
And the other is a prayer.

Here is the secret:
Loving you has made me scandalously beautiful
Did you know when we're apart
the phantom limb of you spasms in me?
How long will that last?

Beat.

  HOLLY. (cont)
Sometimes
I think of you as a grown woman
robust and autonomous
hiking through the snow at night
on your way back from the bars
Your boozy breath in clouds against the night
your cheeks raw from wind and whisky

he's waiting for you back home
He made you coffee
half milk, frothy, in a huge ceramic mug

you whack the snow from your boots
you sit down to the table
and as you raise the hot mug to your lips
you think of a hay ride
A bent hubcap
the color of twilight
cartwheels in a clean patch of grass
stories plowed from the field of your own history

And he watches you drink
And he loves you rigidly, with intention
And I'm so so fucking grateful you get to have this
You get to have everything

So
eat the world, girly
crush it between your molars
suck those rivers dry

and give me the strength to give you the strength
to amplify
forever

>   Beat.

HOLLY. (cont)
that was the prayer.

>   She goos and gahs at the baby.
>   Idiotic mommy noises. They grow
>   bigger and more absurd. She cracks
>   herself up. She cracks the baby up. It
>   goes on. An aria of ridiculous noises
>   punctuated by laughter. Voluminous
>   joy, big and dopey. Then, baby
>   vanishes. Holly turns on a baby
>   monitor and watches the screen,
>   stupid in love.
>
>   Cliff enters in an old-timey bartender
>   uniform—vest, tie, arm garters. He
>   drops to the bed face down, fully
>   clothed.

CLIFF.
Why you still up?

HOLLY.
Gabs has a little fever
She's so cute when she's all sweaty
How was work

CLIFF.
bullshit hours pouring bullshit cocktails for bullshit people
I feel dead

HOLLY.
Better dead than bored, right?

CLIFF.
I'd rather be bored

HOLLY.
No you wouldn't.
Today we spent nine hours at the Mall of America
That's what boredom looks like

CLIFF.
Doing what?

HOLLY.
We rode up and down the escalator like 40 times
I played Q-bert while she napped
We ate three bowls of marbits
That part was kinda magical

CLIFF.
We need to leave this city

HOLLY.
Agreed!

CLIFF.
Let's go to Berlin.

HOLLY.
Ew.

CLIFF.
Why not?
Berlin's "edgy"

HOLLY.
twenty years ago, maybe

CLIFF.
But it's SO CHEAP
Beer costs less than water
I could write all day
I haven't touched my book since the retreat
I could teach Gabi German

CLIFF. (cont)
I could teach *you* German

HOLLY.
I need to learn French first

CLIFF.
And *I* need to figure out how to write like my life depends on it.

HOLLY.
You can't do that somewhere else?

CLIFF.
I wanna be immersed in the native tongue / of my heroes

HOLLY.
(mocking)
"I wanna be immersed in the native tongue of my heroes"

CLIFF.
Ok I'm just gonna say it
I'd really like this.
For us.
Um yeah, cause I…
Kinda…
found this grant on line…
For you

HOLLY.
Me?
Ha!
Get one for yourself.
I'm nobody

CLIFF.
I'm less than nobody

HOLLY.
What kinda grant

CLIFF.
experimental composition

HOLLY.
From where?

CLIFF.
(German accent)
The *Universität der Künste Berlin*

HOLLY.
Say it regular

CLIFF.
The UdK.
Apparently it's like Art Rock Central--

HOLLY.
I know the Udk
thought they didn't take americans.

CLIFF.
Three per year.

HOLLY.
how much is the grant

CLIFF.
A lot

HOLLY.
Enough to live on?

CLIFF.
More.

HOLLY.
For how long?

CLIFF.
A year.

HOLLY.
And housing?

CLIFF.
They'd put us up

HOLLY.
In a kid-friendly place?

CLIFF.
We'd make it kid friendly

HOLLY.
Expenses?

CLIFF.
Covered

                        She thinks. And thinks. And thinks.

CLIFF.
What's the alternative?
We can't afford to go back to New York.
We don't wanna spend another winter here--

HOLLY.
Cliff.
I'm scared.

CLIFF.
Of what?

                        Small beat.

HOLLY.
Of getting everything I want.

CLIFF.
Holly
It's already happening.
Deal with it.

>   Holly vanishes into the bed.

>   Cliff pulls out his laptop. Is lit by its menacing glow. He hits one key over and over. It makes a sound like a buzzer, or an alarm, or an orchestra hit. Rhythmic. A VOICE is heard, in German.

VOICE.
Du bist eine Verschwendung
Du hast kein Leben.
Jedes Potenzial das Du je hattest, hast Du verschwendet.
Wusstest Du, Kafka schrieb "Die Verwandlung", als er neunundzwanzig war?
Und Brecht schrieb "Baal" als er zwanzig war.
Und Du?
Du bist dreißig und Du hast nichts geschrieben.
Du folgst Deiner Frau herum wie ein verlorener Hund
Du bist eine Tragödie.
Du denkst, dass Deine Tochter Dich eines Tages bewundern wird?
Nein, sie wird Dich auslachen.
Sie wird sich fuer Dich schämen.
Sie wird Dir für ihre Sorgen schuld geben.
Und Du wirst Dir jeden Tag gestehen müssen, das nichts aus Dir geworden ist. Herzlichen Glückwunsch, Verlierer.

>   Lights change. Holly emerges from the bed, hops out. Drinks a beer,

                    circling the bed sloppily.

HOLLY.
Still up?

CLIFF.
Was watching some documentary about colonialism
It's insane how people here mythologize the US.
The US didn't invent imperialism for chrisssakes

HOLLY.
We didn't?

CLIFF.
(german accent)
"you've got that frontier spirit, all that open space.
You're always driving, expanding, prevailing--"

HOLLY.
Do any writing?

CLIFF.
I took Gabby to a kindercafe
But I had no cash
ATM kept giving me an error code
So I went to the bank
Wasn't sure how to say "cannot process transaction" in German
So I started speaking English
The lady's like, "I'm sorry, I'm not certified to speak English."
In *English!*
I'm like, "You just did!"
I mean…

HOLLY.
So how did you get money?

                    He holds out his hand. She slaps a
                    bunch of bills in it.

HOLLY.
You make emasculation sexy

CLIFF.
Sweet of you to say
How was your feedback session

HOLLY.
Holy shit holy shit
Cunty Nadia said my songs were "literate and emotionally intricate"

CLIFF.
Wow

HOLLY.
Right?
Oh! Get this.
She asked about our plans
I mentioned we were thinking about LA
She knows this dude in Santa Monica
He's a music supervisor for TV shows
She's gonna send him a few of my / tracks to consider for

CLIFF.
Shhhhhhhh!

> Beat. Holly is confused.

HOLLY.
What?

CLIFF.
Sorry.
Thought I heard Gabs.
Go on.

> Longish beat.

HOLLY.
Um
So
she's gonna send him my stuff
For TV or whatever
Oh then Claude had a show in Friedrichshain
This electroacoustic installation
It was in a fucking converted butcher's
He had speakers in mesh bags / on stands in the corners

CLIFF.
You said fucking.

HOLLY.
What?

CLIFF.
Just please say effing instead.

HOLLY.
Sure thing.

> Holly pulls a pack of smokes from the bed. Shoves a cigarette into her mouth. And another pack. Cigarettes fall from her mouth and litter the bed. She keeps going methodically until she has gone through the whole pack.

CLIFF.
Smoking

HOLLY.
Yup

CLIFF.
Thought you quit

> Holly regards Cliff. Drops the cigarettes. Holds Cliff's hand.

HOLLY.
What's going on with us?

CLIFF.
Nothing. I'm just tired. And you're just drunk.

HOLLY.
Ok
you should get your family to come visit

CLIFF.
It's expensive

HOLLY.
A flight from Paris to Berlin is like a hundred bucks

CLIFF.
We have no room

HOLLY.
We could drag a cot into / Gab's room

CLIFF.
Holly
They won't come

> Holly crushes several handfuls of cigarettes and rubs the tobacco into her hair. She pushes Cliff out of bed. He climbs back in.

HOLLY.
GEEEEET!
UUUUUUUUUUUPPPPPPP!

He doesn't respond. Lights switch.

HOLLY.
I can't find my Xanax

CLIFF.
Why do you need that shit

HOLLY.
I got that interview

CLIFF.
Oh yeah

HOLLY.
They want me to play something

CLIFF.
Play the one from the TV show

HOLLY.
I wanna try something new

CLIFF.
Play the one from the TV show, Holly
It's what they want
They're addicts

HOLLY.
Fine
Fuck I'm a mess.

CLIFF.
So just send the whole house into chaos, why don't you

HOLLY.
What?

CLIFF.
Nothing.

>He closes his eyes again.

>Beat.

HOLLY.
You gonna leave the bed today?

CLIFF.
Interestingly enough I am
Gonna drop Gabs off at school
Wash the car
Water the bushes
Prune the lemon tree
Do the laundry
Clean up the / garage

HOLLY.
PLEASE let me hire people to do that stuff

CLIFF.
Not gonna pay folks to do shit while I sit on my ass

HOLLY.
But you hate it

CLIFF.
So what
needs to get / done

HOLLY.
Thought about Friday yet?

>Cliff groans.

HOLLY.
We're not doing nothing for your birthday, dude

HOLLY. (cont)
Gabs wants to do something

CLIFF.
So we'll do what she wants
I don't want all the fanfare
And NO PRESENTS

HOLLY.
What if I already bought you something?

CLIFF.
Jesus
This is what I mean
It's always what *you* want
You're like a threshing machine
You just hurtle forward
no regard for what you're shredding on the way

                Beat.

I don't mean to sound like a dick

HOLLY.
I know

                Beat.

HOLLY.
I'm gonna go get ready

CLIFF.
I'm going back to sleep

HOLLY.
Ok.

CLIFF.
Good luck today

He closes his eyes. Rolls onto the floor, wrapped up in the sheets. Mummifies himself. Rolls under the bed.

Lights change. Spot on Holly.

HOLLY.
YES!
she just turned six
She's amazing
I'm teaching her how to play the concertina
Such a rad instrument
Used to play one in a punk gypsy band in my 20's
god
we were coked to the gills all tour
Am I allowed to say that on public radio?

Ok, Sorry.
I don't do that anymore, obviously
But one time in hungary
Hungary?
Budapest, Bucharest, don't remember
We got kicked out of this
It was c restaurant
Not fancy or
It was sinister and scuzzy
Like a fried bread hand-job kinda joint?
Some drunk dude by the stage was like
Feeling himself
Not masturbating
kind of absently rolling it around
but he was looking right at me
and I had this like, moment
you know when your eyesight gets kinda sharp
and the noise around you is like
like an animal giving birth?
my blood kinda stopped pumping

HOLLY. (cont)
and I pictured myself leaping off the stage
hurling my body at this loser
shoving my claw down his pants
and tearing his pud right off its stem

So

I went for it
didn't get very far
Like I said I was on drugs
I probably just lunged a little
We didn't get our door money that night
Needless to say

But yeah, I really love being a mom.
Can I play you something now?
It's new
I wrote it for my husband
It's called "Get Up."

> Holly grabs her guitar. Hits a note so she can find her pitch. Sings the following a capella.

I'm gonna skin you alive if you don't get up

I'm gonna eat your soul if you don't get up
I'm gonna I'm gonna ahhhhhhhhhhh....

> Beat. *Caesura.* Holly stands with her guitar. She's now a fucking badass rock star. She surveys the audience, taking them in. Takes her time. Makes eye contact with everyone in the room. She owns them. Smiles as if to say "wait for it, fuckers". Slowly lifts her arm over her head. Pauses. Arm comes crashing down with lights and

> sound as the song kicks in. She plays for a minute.
>
> When she finishes the song, another man emerges from inside the bed. Holly leaps and lands on top of him. They fuck and climax loudly. Holly bursts into tears.

JC.
What, what--

HOLLY.
Sorry
This happens sometimes
With new people

JC.
What should I do

HOLLY.
Nothing.

> Beat as she calms down.

JC.
This is
I mean this is
So.
Fucked.
Up.

HOLLY.
Who's fault is this
Who started it
Was it me?

JC.
Really?

HOLLY.
Oh god
I'm a really bad person

JC.
You are
I just wanna punish you

HOLLY.
There was a supermodel missing some teeth
And I stole something
Didn't I?

JC.
Feral
And your MUSIC!

HOLLY.
Shhhh!
Gabi's asleep—

JC.
Why didn't he tell us you were so fucking good

HOLLY.
It's not really his thing

JC.
It's like Nina Hagen and Petula Clark had a baby
And then they electrocuted her
And she came back as a lady werewolf

HOLLY.
HA HA HA HA!
I think your mom was traumatized--

> He grabs her. They make out. She pulls away.

HOLLY. (cont.)
Fuck
Fuck fuck fuck

JC.
It's ok.
This happens every day
People get through it

HOLLY.
Right

JC.
We've known each other for what
Eight years?
This is a blip

HOLLY.
Right

JC.
In twenty years
we'll laugh our asses off about it

HOLLY.
Right
We'll be like
"Remember the night of my gig at the Mayan
When Cliff took your mom back to her hotel
And we came home and fucked like ferrets?"

JC.
Hilarious

> Beat. His hand slides down her pants.

HOLLY.
Stop stop stop
We were rounding the corner

HOLLY. (cont)
Let's keep up that momentum
"It was great seeing you"

JC.
"Thanks for having me"

HOLLY.
"Have a safe flight back to Paris"

JC.
"Good luck with the tour"

HOLLY.
"Good night"

JC.
"Good night"

>They hug goodnight. For a long long time. They can't let go.

HOLLY.
It'll be ok, right?

JC.
Sure
We care about each other
We're family

HOLLY.
Right

>Cliff climbs out from beneath the bed. He is lit eerily. Panic.

CLIFF.
At this moment
I picture Holly's giant, terrified eyes coming at me

CLIFF. (cont)
All blown out like old tires
She shrieks
"When did they burst? Did you hear them burst?"
I'm like
"I can't hear anything!
Gabi's laughter is chiming up and down my spine!"

And she goes:
"You're dragging those fucking chimes up and down your spine yourself!
You're letting them bury you down into silence
Because you've become too heavy to hold yourself up!"

And I'm like
"Didn't we promise to hold each other up?
Wasn't that the deal?"

And she goes....

"You're too heavy for both of us now."

>   Small beat.

CLIFF. (cont)
I don't know what I'm doing. I don't know what I'm doing.

> He climbs back under the bed.

> Lights shift. Holly and JC are fucking again. They both climax.

HOLLY.
Simultaneous, bitches!!

> JC rolls over and lights a cigarette. Offers her one. She takes it. He lights it for her.

JC.
You're fun

HOLLY.
Yeah

JC.
Do you mind if I make a phone call?

HOLLY.
It's your apartment

> JC makes a phone call.

JC.
Allo.
Oui, je suis chez moi.
Je ne peux pas, je suis occupe avec le restaurant ce matin
Il peut passer le temps la bas avec moi.
Mais, que-ce-que tu veuilles que je fasse? Je dois travailler.
Tu es déplaisant quand tu lances des accusations comme ca.
J'en ai pas de patience pour ca maintenant.
Bon. D'accord.

> He hangs up.

HOLLY.
That your wife?

JC.
How could you tell?

HOLLY.
Something about your tone.

JC.
She uses our son as a bargaining tool
It's unappealing

JC. (cont)
I don't want to talk about her
How long are you in Paris?

HOLLY.
Til Sunday

JC.
Aw.
Too bad

HOLLY.
Then Oslo, Copenhagen, Stockholm, / Milan, Vienna, Lisbon, blah blah...

JC.
Brag brag brag

HOLLY.
I'll be back Strasbourg in a month
Feel like driving east?

JC.
Can't leave the restaurant

HOLLY.
make it a work trip
Sample some wines
Taste some forbidden fruit

> She licks his fingers. He nuzzles into her, sniffs her like an animal. Growls.

JC.
Can't get enough of you
Your smell
Like a bleeding dog in the dead of summer

> He burrows into her. Her alarm goes

off.

HOLLY.
Shit
I told Cliff and Gabs I'd Skype with them at eight
He gets pissy when I'm late

JC.
You know we called him The Mope growing up
Had this ratty journal he'd carry around
Thought he was gonna be famous by the time he turned 20

HOLLY.
What happened

JC.
Nothing
No one gets to be famous by 20
People work hard for the shit they want
It's strenuous, it's harrowing
And then? It's over

HOLLY.
Then why do it?

JC.
To have a constant spiny reminder of our own humanity
Extreme pain does that
Not everyone has the stomach for it

HOLLY.
Do you?

JC.
I do.
So do you.

                      Beat. Holly's alarm goes off again.

JC. (cont)
Skype him.

HOLLY.
from here?
Sure

JC.
I'm sure he assumes you'd visit me
Put your top on
Tell him I stepped out to get croissants

HOLLY.
And where will you be

JC.
Beneath the covers
Getting you off.

JC pulls out a computer from the bed and hands it to Holly. Then dives beneath the covers. Holly puts on her top and grabs her phone and headphones. Opens the Skype app. Types a little.

Cliff is projected somewhere. He's huge.

HOLLY.
Hey.

CLIFF.
Hi.

HOLLY.
Where's Gabi?

CLIFF.
In her room
Maddie's over
They're playing "car crash vicitim"
She always wants to be the decapitated nun

HOLLY.
I love that little fucking weirdo

CLIFF.
Where are you?

HOLLY.
At JC.'s!

CLIFF.
Oh great!
he there?

HOLLY.
He stepped out for food

CLIFF.
What's his place like?

HOLLY.
Nice
He has good taste

CLIFF.
Are you staying there?

HOLLY.
Nah
Just here for dinner

CLIFF.
Quick visit

HOLLY.
He's busy

CLIFF.
Has he pissed you off yet?

HOLLY.
Not yet
We're getting along this time

> JC does something extreme beneath the covers. Holly gasps, then covers.

CLIFF.
Are you ok?

HOLLY.
Yeah, sorry
I'm fine

CLIFF.
Ok

> Beat. Cliff searches... feeling lost...

CLIFF. (cont)
Um
Oh!
Know what I was thinking about today?
Remember that time at the laundromat
In Minneapolis

HOLLY.
Which time

CLIFF.
I was reading a book about aestheticism and performativity

CLIFF. (cont)
I tried to explain something
"Kalfka seeks to deterritorialize the linguistic hierarchy
andduuuuuuhhhhhhhhh buh buh buh buh"
I had a stroke, or

HOLLY.
HA!
Oh my god--

CLIFF.
You laughed so hard
a blood vessel burst in your nose
But you couldn't stop
You were laughing and bleeding
We had to wash all the sheets again

HOLLY.
Nasty fucking shit--

CLIFF.
I miss you
I miss you.

>   Beat. Holly is surprised and moved.
>   Lights change. JC emerges from
>   inside the bed. Hotel bed. They both
>   wear cocktail party clothes. They're
>   both drunk.

HOLLY.
Where the fuck is the fucking minibar
Jesus

JC.
Yikes
Why so ragey?

HOLLY.
Really?

JC.
You looked beautiful
You behaved well
I was knowledgeable and charming
And my food was beyond reproach
a radiant success, all told

HOLLY.
You had your arm around me the whole event
That dude thinks we're fucking
The venture capitalist--

JC.
WE ARE FUCKING.
NO ONE CARES.

HOLLY.
I care.
We're not in Paris
It could get back to Cliff

JC.
He has no one in New York anymore

HOLLY.
There were *photographers*--

JC.
Let me tell you what I believe, Holly
I believe in moral relativism
The ability to relate
And the desire for empathy
All else is pettiness.

HOLLY.
As if other people don't actually exist

JC.
Those who judge others for acting within their nature
Are refusing to acknowledge the full spectrum of human desire

HOLLY.
And YOU are refusing to acknowledge that what you say
And how you act
Might actually affect people's lives

JC.
Maybe I just don't give a fuck

HOLLY.
Nice

JC.
I understand you're emotional
It happens, it's ok
But don't make me feel like I've made a mistake
You're more evolved than that.

HOLLY.
"Evolved"
Ok.
I'm fucking evolved.

JC.
Then act like it.

HOLLY.
Suck. My. Dick.

JC.
Aw.
That's cute.
There's nothing complicated about what we're doing, kid
Keep that in mind and everything will be swell.

> Grabs a flask, pours her a shot.

JC. (cont)
Now.
Let's celebrate
To my tiny feral post-punk prodigy
Thank you for meeting me in New York
Thank you for accompanying me to this potentially life-changing career event
Thank you for lying to your family to do so--

HOLLY.
Your family
They're your family too

> Beat.

JC. (cont)
Remember we said we'd pull the plug when this stopped being fun?

HOLLY.
Don't

JC.
It's time

HOLLY.
Don't
Don't
Don't
Don't
Don't
Don't
Don't
Don't
Don't

JC disappears into the bed.

Holly grabs her guitar. Lights slowly change. The following is part song part spoken.

   HOLLY.
Ha!

And you were like, "I like evil girls!"
And I was like, "I'm pretty fucking evil"
And you were like, "ok, no not evil, really"
And I was like, "I'm actually not evil I'm just confused"
And you were like, "no I meant evil, I was right the first time"
And I was like, "now I'm confused and I'm still evil"

And you were like, "ok let's get real"

You were like, "evil is fun to fuck but gets to be a bit much"
And I was like, "I can be a bit much, sure, but"

And I was like, "you said you have the stomach for it"
And I was like, "what about moral relativism"
And you were like, "evilness is not good. I just realized."
And I was like, "what do I have left"
And I was like, "I have nothing"
And you were like, "oops"

Ha!

Well baby, are you bored?
Better dead than bored

Hey
Hey JC.
Your brother is a smarter dude
Your brother is a better lay

And I was out the fuckin' door anyway

>   Something's wrong. She can't finish
>   the song. Tries again.

HOLLY. (cont)
And I was out the fuckin' door--
No... fuck.

>   Still wrong. Tries again.

HOLLY. (cont)
AND I WAS OUT THE FUCKIN' DOOR ANYWAY

>   Tries something different. It sucks.
>   She's pissed, confused, etc. Beat.
>
>   Cliff emerges from within the bed.

CLIFF.
Hey
How's the song coming

HOLLY.
It's not

CLIFF.
You'll get there

HOLLY.
You said that last week
And the week before.

CLIFF.
Because it's true

HOLLY.
It's been a month
I don't know what I'm doing

CLIFF.
Maybe you need a break--

HOLLY.
I don't need a break
I need to finish it
…
How are you feeling

CLIFF.
Pretty good, actually
I think the meds are actually fucking working

HOLLY.
You said fucking! Yay!

CLIFF.
I did
I'm fixed!

HOLLY.
Did your family notice

CLIFF.
Not really
It's actually a bearable visit
Dad and I had a big ol' chat last night
Seemed almost proud of me

HOLLY.
About the job?
Does he know it's just adjunct work?

CLIFF.
He said he didn't care
As long as I'm happy
He was kind of drunk
JC. kept ordering rounds of high end scotch
Those Michelin stars went straight to his head

HOLLY.
Guess we should check his place out

CLIFF.
Not my kind of food
Gabby might like it though

HOLLY.
She's so weird!
What nine-year-old likes *foie gras*?

CLIFF.
JC was pretty wasted too
Haven't seen him that drunk since our wedding

HOLLY.
What'd you guys talk about?

CLIFF.
My marriage
Asked how it was going

HOLLY.
What did you say

CLIFF.
I said we hit a rough patch a while back
But we've been doing pretty good lately
He seemed happy to hear it
He'd been worried

HOLLY.
Why?

CLIFF.
You know
He was always worried about you screwing me over

HOLLY.
Oh.
That's rude--

CLIFF.
He also told me you cried the first time he fucked you

>Beat.

CLIFF. (cont)
I was pretty shocked
About the fucking, not the crying
I asked a bunch of questions
Was it just once, were you drunk

He told me
Los Angeles
Paris
New York
Drunk
Sober
Awake
Said it was your idea
But he kept it going
He felt bad
Said it was a mistake

HOLLY.
Cliff—

CLIFF.
He said it was eating him up
was afraid you'd spill the beans first
He thinks you're unstable
I was like
"she's not unstable
she's an artist!"

>Beat.

HOLLY.
(quiet)
What else did he say

CLIFF.
He's not lying, Holly
Is he

          Beat. Holly says nothing.

CLIFF. (cont)
Ok.

          Cliff tries to make a decision to leave. Starts to pack a bag.

CLIFF. (cont)
I fucking...
I don't know how to forgive him
I don't know how to forgive you--

HOLLY.
I don't want forgiveness

CLIFF.
What do you want

HOLLY.
Punishment.

          Longish beat.

CLIFF.
No...

HOLLY.
You knew this.
You knew this about me.

CLIFF.
Holly--

HOLLY.
You've always known.
...
Go on.

> She waits. Cliff can't move. Long beat.

HOLLY.
Pathetic--

CLIFF.
Why? 'Cause I won't hurt you?

HOLLY.
Because you allowed yourself to die inside a living body
And you won't take responsibility / for it

CLIFF.
On *your* terms!
Everything's always on / your terms!

HOLLY.
You don't have any terms of your own!
Name one!
Name *one fucking thing* you / want.

CLIFF.
The absence of chaos.

HOLLY.
Is that a joke?

> Beat. Cliff doesn't know what to say. Holly grabs a suitcase from inside the

> bed and throws everything into it.

CLIFF.
Oh now *you're* leaving.
Of course.
Stupid me, what was I thinking

> Then, she starts throwing child stuff into it.

CLIFF.
You're packing her shit too? Great.
Fuck!
Ok here's some "wants":
I want be the one to leave for once!
I want you to not have fucked my brother
I want some goddamn dignity

HOLLY.
(small)
Why don't you want what you threw away?

> Beat.

CLIFF.
You?

> She nods.

CLIFF. (cont)
I do
I just don't / know how to

HOLLY.
Then punish me.

CLIFF.
Holly--

HOLLY.
Punish me, you piece of shit

CLIFF.
I don't punish

HOLLY.
Then fight for me

CLIFF.
I don't fight

HOLLY.
Then fight for her!

CLIFF.
How?

HOLLY.
By punishing me.

                    Long beat.

CLIFF.
(weakly)
What should I do?

HOLLY.
Figure it out.

                    Beat. Cliff searches the bed. Filled with trepidation. Pulls a gun from inside the bed. Closes his eyes. He shoots her in the face. She falls, then gets back up.

CLIFF.
Why didn't it work?

>Holly can't help him. He pulls out a larger gun. He shoots her in the face. She falls, then gets back up.

CLIFF. (cont)
What the fuck?

>Beat. He pulls out a bazooka. Gestures for her to back up a little. Aims the bazooka at her face. Shoots her. She goes down. Doesn't get up this time.
>
>Beat.

CLIFF. (cont)
Are you dead yet?

HOLLY.
kinda

CLIFF.
What do I do now

HOLLY.
You jerk off on me

CLIFF.
Why

HOLLY.
You know why

CLIFF.
You weren't dead when he did it

HOLLY.
Yes I was
I was dead the whole time

>Beat. He unzips. Starts to jerk off on her.

CLIFF.
Say you love yourself

HOLLY.
I don't

CLIFF.
Say it
Otherwise I / can't do this

HOLLY.
Fine. I love myself

CLIFF.
Louder

HOLLY.
I LOVE MYSELF

CLIFF.
You're a good person

HOLLY.
I'M A GOOD PERSON

CLIFF.
Why?

HOLLY.
What?

CLIFF.
Say why!

>Holly shouts.

HOLLY.
OK!
I'M FUN-LOVING!
I'M LOYAL!
I'M A DECENT MOM!
UM…

CLIFF.
What about music?

HOLLY.
I HAVE GREAT RHYTHM!
I HAVE PERFECT PITCH!
I PICK UP INSTRUMENTS QUICKLY!
MY TASTE IS IMPECCABLE!
I CAN SHRED LIKE A DEMON!
I…
JESUS…

CLIFF.
Your hair!

HOLLY.
I HAVE… SHINY HAIR!
I CAN CURL MY TONGUE!
MY MOUTH IS PRETTY!
MY CHEEKBONES ARE FRIENDLY!
MY THIGHS ARE FANTASTIC!
MY CLAVICLE IS DELICATE!
UM…

CLIFF.
Personality!

HOLLY.
I'M KIND-HEARTED!
I'M GENEROUS!
I'M AN EXCELLENT LISTENER!

HOLLY. (cont)
I'M CALM IN A CRISIS!
THAT'S NOT TRUE!
I HAVE GOOD COMIC TIMING!
I DON'T SUFFER FOOLS!
UNLESS THEY'RE ENTERTAINING!
I'M...
I TIP WELL!
I...
I...

CLIFF.
KEEP GOING!

HOLLY.
I..
HAVE...
AN...
AUTHORITATIVE...
HANDSHAKE...

>He finishes on her. Hands her a towel.
>She wipes off. Long beat.

CLIFF.
You ok?

HOLLY.
Dunno.

CLIFF.
gonna laugh?

HOLLY.
No.

CLIFF.
Cry?

HOLLY.
No.

CLIFF.
stop living like you're being hunted?

> Small beat.

HOLLY.
No.

> Beat.

HOLLY.
What about you?
Still dead?

> Long long beat.

CLIFF.
Better dead than bored.

> Beat.

> He smiles. That was a joke, kinda. She gets it. Blackout.

END OF PLAY.

OUT THE DOOR

kind-er soul   Your bro-ther is a bet-ter lay, And I was out the fuck in' door

G⁵   C⁵

a - ny - way.___ And I was out the fuck-in' door a - ny - way.___ And

G⁵

I was out the fuck - in' door a - ny - way

C⁵

increase strumming intensity (she's shredding now)

A⁵

Made in the USA
Middletown, DE
13 December 2020